PRODIGALS
AND THOSE
WHO LOVE THEM

STUDY GUIDE

PRODIGALS
AND THOSE
WHO LOVE THEM

STUDY GUIDE

STEPHEN GRIFFITH AND BILL DECKARD

PUBLISHING
Colorado Springs, Colorado

STUDY GUIDE: PRODIGALS AND THOSE WHO LOVE THEM

Editor: Janet Kobobel
Designer: Sherry Nicolai Russell
Cover illustration: Joe Van Severen

Printed in the United States of America
92 93 94 95 96 / 10 9 8 7 6 5 4 3 2

CONTENTS

INTRODUCTION

At Focus on the Family we work hard to prepare tools to help heal the hurts we see in families today. We've known for quite a while that many were dealing with prodigals—sons, daughters, wives, husbands, brothers, sisters. We also knew a book that encouraged and helped those who loved a prodigal could not be written by just anyone. So we waited until we found the right person.

That individual turned out to be Ruth Bell Graham. Her book offers a wealth of wisdom from her own life, from the lives of several prodigals through history and from the wide reading and studying she has done on the subject.

This study guide is a supplement to Mrs. Graham's book. Working through this guide will help you mine the depths of the Bible as well as her book. By taking the main themes that run throughout Mrs. Graham's book and relating them to certain Bible passages, we've tried to provide practical helps to those with a prodigal. For those hurting individuals, no better medicine exists than to immerse themselves in Scripture, to learn more of God and to meditate on how His truths can help today.

May you find the following material a healing balm.

LESSON ONE

No Condemnation: God's Grace

"REMIND THEM GENTLY, LORD, HOW YOU

HAVE TROUBLE WITH YOUR CHILDREN, TOO."

—FROM "THEY FELT GOOD EYES UPON THEM" BY RUTH BELL GRAHAM

IN *PRODIGALS AND THOSE WHO LOVE THEM*

I

n Prodigals and Those Who Love Them, Mrs. Graham chooses not to condemn the prodigal for several reasons. First, she knows God is the judge and will make His judgment in His own time. Second, she can hate the sin yet love the sinner. And third, since all have sinned, prodigals are no more worthy of condemnation than the rest of us.

The passages below show some of the foundation for such thinking.

BIBLE PASSAGES

"There is no one righteous, not even one; there is no one who understands, no one who seeks God. All have turned away, they have together become worthless; there is no one who does good, not even one" (Romans 3:10-12).

"Therefore, just as sin entered the world through one man, and death through sin, and in this way death came to all men, because all sinned" (Romans 5:12).

YOUR INSIGHTS

1. In the above verses, Paul paints a bleak portrait of the human race. How does your own experience with people compare to it?

2. The "one man" through whom sin entered the world (5:12) was Adam. What evidence does Paul present to prove we all inherited Adam's sinful nature?

3. Can you recall a time when you were tempted to exclude yourself from the "all" of 5:12? Why do you think you were tempted to do so?

BIBLE PASSAGES

"But the gift is not like the trespass. For if the many died by the trespass of the one man, how much more did God's grace and the gift that came by the grace of the one man, Jesus Christ, overflow to the many!" (Romans 5:15).

"For it is by grace you have been saved, through faith—and this not from yourselves, it is the gift of God—not by works, so that no one can boast" (Ephesians 2:8-9).

YOUR INSIGHTS

4. We received our sin nature from Adam. What does Paul say we can receive through Jesus Christ?

5. Paul refers to righteousness as a "gift." How can understanding this truth keep us from being self-righteous?

6. According to the Ephesians passage, where does believing faith come from?

7. Can you recall ever boasting about works you have done? How did you feel when you were boasting?

PRODIGALS AND THOSE WHO LOVE THEM

Marget's heart burned within her at the sight, and she could hardly make allowance for Lachlan's blood and theology. "This is what you have done, and you let a woman see your work. You are an old man, and in sore travail, but I tell you before God, you have the greater shame. Just twenty years o' age this spring, and her mother dead. No woman to watch over her, and she wandered from the fold, and all you can do is to take her out o' your Bible. Woe is me if our Father had blotted out our names from the Book o' Life when we left His house. But He sent His Son to seek us, an' a weary road He came. I tell you, a man would not leave a sheep to perish as you have cast off your own child. You're worse than Simon the Pharisee, for Mary was not kin to him. Poor Flora, to have such a father."

—from "Flora Campbell" in *Prodigals and Those Who Love Them*

Read the chapter "Flora Campbell" is its entirety.

8. Because Flora left home, her father crossed her name out of the family Bible and said his daughter lived no more. What emotions do you think Lachlan felt when he made these choices? Circle your answers below, and add those feelings you do not see listed.

grief   anger   embarrassment   fear for self
fear for Flora   guilt   other: _____
_____

9. Go back to the list, and put a larger circle around the emotions you have felt about having a prodigal in your life.

10. Read the story of Simon the Pharisee in Luke 7:36-50. In what ways is Simon the Pharisee like Lachlan? Do you recognize any aspects of the Pharisee in yourself?

11. When Marget rebuked Lachlan, how did she use Christ as an example for Lachlan to follow? How does that help you to view your prodigal?

BIBLE PASSAGES

"My sheep listen to my voice; I know them, and they follow me. I give them eternal life, and they shall never perish; no one can snatch them out of my hand" (John 10:27-28).

"My prayer is not that you [God] take them out of the world but that you protect them from the evil one. They are not of the world, even as I am not of it. Sanctify them by the truth; your word is truth" (John 17:15-17).

YOUR INSIGHTS

12. According to John 10:27, what characterizes Christians?

13. Who, according to verse 28, should primarily get the credit for our staying faithful to Christ?

14. In John 17, where did Jesus say we get the ability to resist the temptations all around us? How is this another demonstration of God's grace?

BIBLE PASSAGE

"This is the message we have heard from him and declare to you: God is light; in him there is no darkness at all. If we claim to have fellowship with him yet walk in the darkness, we lie and do not live by the truth. But if we walk in the light, as he is in the light, we have fellowship with one another, and the blood of Jesus, his Son, purifies us from all sin.

"If we claim to be without sin, we deceive ourselves and the truth is not in us. If we confess our sins, he is faithful and just and will forgive us our sins and purify us from all unrighteousness" (1 John 1:5-9).

YOUR INSIGHTS
15. In what ways are Christians like "light" instead of "darkness"?

16. Verse 5 says there is "no darkness at all" in God. How do Christians differ from God in that regard, according to the passage?

17. According to these verses, what should we do when we find areas of darkness in our lives?

PRODIGALS AND THOSE WHO LOVE THEM

THEY FELT GOOD EYES UPON THEM

They felt good eyes upon them
and shrank within—undone;
good parents had good children
and they—a wandering one.

The good folk never meant
to act smug or condemn,
but having prodigals
just "wasn't done" with them.

* * *

Remind them gently, Lord,
how You
have trouble with Your children,
too.

—Ruth Bell Graham

18. Recall times when you've said or thought to yourself, "XX's parents don't take good care of him" or " I'm glad I'm not like that."

19. In the situation you face, are you concentrating on the faults of the other person more than on your own? How might an adjustment of your thinking bring relief and a more accurate picture of the situation?

SUMMARY

When someone close to you leaves home or rebels against authority in some way, disappointment, sorrow and even anger can become your dominant emotions, because your focus is on them and their faults. It's important to remember at such times that we have all been prodigals from God.

PRACTICING HIS GRACE: FORGIVENESS AND MERCY

THIS KNOWLEDGE OF WHAT HE HAD BEEN WAS ALWAYS WITH

NEWTON AND WAS THE SOURCE OF HIS POWER IN PREACHING

GOD'S GRACE—FOR HE HAD TASTED IT HIMSELF.

—FROM "JOHN NEWTON" IN *PRODIGALS AND THOSE WHO LOVE THEM*

MRS. Graham's book is more about what the Lord did in her life than it is about the details of her experience with prodigals. She shows us that being beneficiaries of God's saving grace should have a profound impact on us, especially on how we treat other people. His grace should instill in us an attitude of understanding and forgiveness. But what does that mean with regard to our prodigals?

BIBLE PASSAGE

"Then Peter came to Jesus and asked, 'Lord, how many times shall I forgive my brother when he sins against me? Up to seven times?'

"Jesus answered, 'I tell you, not seven times, but seventy-seven times'" (Matthew 18:21-22).

YOUR INSIGHTS

1. How do you think Peter expected Jesus to respond to his question?

2. What did Jesus mean by His answer? (Some translations say "seventy times seven." What actual number do you think Jesus had in mind?)

3. Is there anyone whom you have forgiven "seventy-seven times"? What have you learned from that experience? What signs of change have you seen in the forgiven person?

BIBLE PASSAGE

"Therefore, the kingdom of heaven is like a king who wanted to settle accounts with his servants. As he began the settlement, a man who owed him ten thousand talents was brought to him. Since he was not able to pay, the master ordered that he and his wife and his children and all that he had be sold to repay the debt.

"The servant fell on his knees before him. 'Be patient with me,' he begged, 'and I will pay back everything.' The servant's master took pity on him, canceled the debt and let him go.

"But when that servant went out, he found one of his fellow servants who owed him a hundred denarii. He grabbed him and began to choke him. 'Pay back what you owe me!' he demanded.

"His fellow servant fell to his knees and begged him, 'Be patient with me, and I will pay you back.'

"But he refused. . . .

"Then the master called the servant in. 'You wicked servant,' he said, 'I canceled all that debt of yours because you begged me to. Shouldn't you have had mercy on your fellow servant just as I had on you?' In anger his master turned him over to the jailers . . . until he should pay back all he owed.

"This is how my heavenly Father will treat each of you unless you forgive your brother from your heart" (Matthew 18:23-30, 32-35).

YOUR INSIGHTS

4. The first servant owed the king millions more than his fellow servant owed him. Why is this a key fact in the story?

5. How does the huge amount of the ungrateful servant's debt correspond to our relationship with God?

6. Jesus told this parable right after He told Peter to forgive seventy-seven times. What does it add to your understanding of His command?

7. In light of this parable, what should our attitude be toward people who have wronged us or failed to live up to our expectations?

PRODIGALS AND THOSE WHO LOVE THEM

William Jay, another minister, tells the story of calling on Newton one day and hearing Newton say, "I am glad to see you, for I have just received a letter from Bath, and you may know something of the writer," mentioning his name.

Jay told him he did indeed know the writer and that he was the most awful character.

"But," says Newton, "he writes now like a penitent."

"He may be such," Jay said, "but, if he be, I shall never despair of the conversion of anyone again."

"Oh," said Newton, "I never did, since God saved me."

—From "John Newton" in *Prodigals and Those Who Love Them*

Please reread the chapter "John Newton."

8. What character trait does John Newton display in the above anecdote?

9. Think about someone you know who has sinned against you or God. How do you think Newton would respond to that person? Do you treat that person in the same way?

10. What characteristic of John Newton would you like to be more true of your own life? How can you begin to incorporate it into your experience?

BIBLE PASSAGE

"Get rid of all bitterness, rage and anger, brawling and slander, along with every form of malice. Be kind and compassionate to one another, forgiving each other, just as in Christ God forgave you" (Ephesians 4:31-32).

YOUR INSIGHTS

11. How can the characteristics in the first sentence of the above verse hamper your relationship with God?

12. What does Paul imply is the key to overcoming such barriers?

BIBLE PASSAGE

"If anyone has caused grief, he has not so much grieved me as he has grieved all of you, to some extent—not to put it too severely. The punishment inflicted on him by the majority is sufficient for him. Now instead, you ought to forgive and comfort him, so that he will not be overwhelmed by excessive sorrow. I urge you, therefore, to reaffirm your love for him" (2 Corinthians 2:5-8).

YOUR INSIGHTS

13. We don't know the full story behind this note to the Corinthian church, but we can assume that "he" had wronged the church and been duly punished. What course of action does Paul now recommend?

14. What does Paul say could result from lack of forgiveness in this situation?

15. Why is it often hard to follow discipline with forgiveness?

16. Think of a time when you were delighted to see someone "get what was coming" to him or her. How might an appreciation of God's grace modify your response?

PRODIGALS AND THOSE WHO LOVE THEM

OUR FAILURES

Colleen Evans, in her challenging book *Start Loving,* quotes a friend who had written her:

Our failures. That's the hardest area, especially when they have affected the lives of our loved ones. As our two children step out into the adult world it is a joy to see many beautiful things in their lives. But it hurts to see areas of need and struggle that stem in part from ways we have failed them.

A friend reminded me recently that even these areas are part of the "all things" which God will use to make a man and a woman who will accomplish His unique purposes.

So when thoughts of my failures push their way into my consciousness, I let His total forgiveness dissolve my regrets, and go on to praise Him who accepts us just as we are and lovingly works to make us more than we are.

And from the same book, "He doesn't expect us—or our children—to be finished products now."

—From *Prodigals and Those Who Love Them*

17. In Colleen Evans's quote, how did she avoid condemning her children for those areas of "need" they had?

18. How can you apply her remarks to your situation and need?

SUMMARY

John Newton's life illustrates how God instills an attitude of understanding and forgiveness. Newton knew that if God could save him, He could save anyone. Like Newton, we need to show love and understanding to others because we've been received by God.

LESSON THREE

GOD'S SUSTAINING LOVE

I LOVE YOU DEARLY, BUT MY LOVE IS NOTHING

COMPARED WITH THE LOVE OF GOD.

—DOSTOYEVSKI TO HIS CHILDREN FROM

PRODIGALS AND THOSE WHO LOVE THEM

L

L_OVE_ is a word often thrown around with little meaning. But God doesn't throw it around.

BIBLE PASSAGE

"The LORD did not set his affection on you and choose you because you were more numerous than other peoples, for you were the fewest of all peoples. But it was because the LORD loved you and kept the oath he swore to your forefathers that he brought you out with a mighty hand and redeemed you from the land of slavery, from the power of Pharaoh king of Egypt. Know therefore that the LORD your God is God; he is the faithful God, keeping his covenant of love to a thousand generations of those who love him and keep his commands" (Deuteronomy 7:7-9).

YOUR INSIGHTS

1. Why did God choose Israel as His people? How does His reason reassure us?

2. What does the passage tell us about the characteristics of His love?

BIBLE PASSAGES

"I revealed myself to those who did not ask for me; I was found by those who did not seek me. To a nation that did not call on my name, I said, 'Here am I, here am I.' All day long I have held out my hands to an obstinate people, who walk in ways not good, pursuing their own imaginations" (Isaiah 65:1-2).

"O Jerusalem, Jerusalem, you who kill the prophets and stone those sent to you, how often I have longed to gather your children together, as a hen gathers her chicks under her wings, but you were not willing" (Matthew 23:37).

YOUR INSIGHTS

3. What does the verse from Isaiah show us about God's love?

4. Centuries later, as recorded in Matthew, God's people are still not responding to His love. What is the problem?

5. What are the implications of these verses regarding how God views your prodigal?

BIBLE PASSAGE

"God was reconciling the world to himself in Christ" (2 Corinthians 5:19a).

YOUR INSIGHTS

6. What does the word *reconcile* mean? Why do we need to be reconciled to God?

7. How does God's desire for this reconciliation show His love for us?

8. Explain how Christ was God's ultimate means of seeking reconciliation with His people.

9. What does this verse tell you God is willing to do to reconcile with your prodigal?

BIBLE PASSAGES

"For God so loved the world that he gave his one and only Son, that whoever believes in him shall not perish but have eternal life. For God did not send his Son into the world to condemn the world, but to save the world through him" (John 3:16-17).

"You see, at just the right time, when we were still powerless, Christ died for the ungodly. Very rarely will anyone die for a righteous man, though for a good man someone might possibly dare to die. But God demonstrates his own love for us in this: While we were still sinners, Christ died for us" (Romans 5:6-8).

YOUR INSIGHTS

10. How does Christ's death demonstrate His love for us? How does it demonstrate the Father's love?

11. What do these verses tell us about our condition when Christ died for us?

12. What did we deserve, instead of God's love?

13. How do these thoughts sustain you as you wait for your prodigal's return?

PRODIGALS AND THOSE WHO LOVE THEM

Read the hymn "In Tenderness He Sought Me" on page 73 in Mrs. Graham's book.

14. What characteristics of God's love do you find in this hymn?

15. How did God seek you? How do you think God is seeking your prodigal?

16. Do you agree with Mrs. Graham's thought at the end of the hymn? Why or why not?

BIBLE PASSAGE

"Who shall separate us from the love of Christ? Shall trouble or hardship or persecution or famine or nakedness or danger or sword? As it is written:

" 'For your sake we face death all day long; we are considered as sheep to be slaughtered.'

"No, in all these things we are more than conquerors through him who loved us. For I am convinced that neither death nor life, neither angels nor demons, neither the present nor the future, nor any powers, neither height nor depth, nor anything else in all creation, will be able to separate us from the love of God that is in Christ Jesus our Lord" (Romans 8:35-39).

YOUR INSIGHTS

17. How does Christ's love help us be "more than conquerors" amid all the hardships Paul describes?

18. Circle the things Paul mentioned in the above verses that have tried to separate you from God's love. Have they ever succeeded in doing so?

PRODIGALS AND THOSE WHO LOVE

I BRING THOSE WHOM I LOVE

I bring those whom I love
to You,
commit each to
Your loving care:
then carry them away again
nor leave them there:
forgetting You
Who lived to die
(and rose again!)
care more than I.

So back I come
with my heart's load,
confessing
my lack of faith
in You alone,
addressing
all I cannot understand

to You
Who do.
You know each heart,
each hidden wound,
each scar,
each one who played a part
in making those
we bring to You
the ones they are
(and dearer each to You
than us, by far),

So—
now I give them
to Your loving care,
with thankful heart,
—and leave them there.

—Ruth Bell Graham

19. What comment is Mrs. Graham making about God's love in this poem?

20. How has she responded (or failed to respond) to God's love?

21. How has your response to God's love been similar to or different from Mrs. Graham's?

GOD! THOU ART LOVE!

God! Thou art Love! I build my faith on that! . . .
I know Thee, who has kept my path, and made
Light for me in the darkness—tempering sorrow,
So that it reached me like a solemn joy;
It were too strange that I should doubt Thy love . . .

—Robert Browning from Paracelsus in
Prodigals and Those Who Love Them

22. Why does Browning think doubting God's love would be a strange response?

23. How has the love of God been evident in your own life? Has He been faithful "in the darkness"?

24. How can the past help you to believe God loves you now?

SUMMARY

God has always been a loving Father. Meditating on His everlasting love should help us cope with a world filled with sometimes-less-than-loving people, as well as give us the security that love brings.

IMITATING HIS LOVE

WHOM MY HEART CHERISHES ARE DEAR TO THY HEART TOO

—FROM "LOVE KNOWS WHAT TO DO" BY AMY CARMICHAEL

IN *PRODIGALS AND THOSE WHO LOVE THEM*

I

IF God's love sustains us and woos our prodigal back to Him, what can happen in our lives and the lives of our prodigals if we become reflections of His love?

BIBLE PASSAGES

". . . So that Christ may dwell in your hearts through faith. And I pray that you, being rooted and established in love, may have power, together with all the saints, to grasp how wide and long and high and deep is the love of Christ, and to know this love that surpasses knowledge—that you may be filled to the measure of all the fullness of God" (Ephesians 3:17-19).

"Be imitators of God, therefore, as dearly loved children and live a life of love, just as Christ loved us and gave himself up for us as a fragrant offering and sacrifice to God" (Ephesians 5:1-2).

YOUR INSIGHTS

1. As Christians, what should motivate us to show love to others?

2. What lesser motives sometimes guide us to either give or withhold love?

3. What does Paul say about God's love that could give us more courage to take risks in loving people who may not return our love?

4. What are some practical ways we can become "imitators of God" in relating to the people in our lives, especially our prodigals?

BIBLE PASSAGE

"If I speak in the tongues of men and of angels, but have not love, I am only a resounding gong or a clanging cymbal. If I have the gift of prophecy and can fathom all mysteries and all knowledge, and if I have a faith that can move mountains, but have not love, I am nothing. If I give all I possess to the poor and surrender my body to the flames, but have not love, I gain nothing.

"Love is patient, love is kind. It does not envy, it does not boast, it is not proud. It is not rude, it is not self-seeking, it is not easily angered, it keeps no record of wrongs. Love does not delight in evil but rejoices with the truth. It always protects, always trusts, always hopes, always perseveres" (1 Corinthians 13:1-7).

YOUR INSIGHTS

5. How can Paul's perspective in the first paragraph of the above passage help you in knowing how to reach out to a spiritually needy person?

6. Paul seems to say that love is better than always having the right answer. Do you agree? Why or why not?

7. Paul also says that good works without love gain us nothing in God's eyes. How well can others tell when our good deeds are done without love?

8. Make a checklist of the qualities of love Paul describes in the second half of the passage. Put an "x" by your strong points. Place a check mark by your weaker points. Ask God to help you to improve in your weaker areas.

9. When dealing with a prodigal, it's all too easy to "keep a record of wrongs." How can Paul's words help you resist this tendency?

10. How can each of the "always" items in the last sentence of the passage help you while you wait for a loved one's return?

PRODIGALS AND THOSE WHO LOVE THEM

IF I COULD STAND ASIDE

If I could stand aside
and see
him walking through
Those Splendor'd Gates
thrown wide,
instead of me—
If I could yield my place
to this, my boy,
the tears upon my upturned face
would be
of joy!

—Ruth Bell Graham

11. What characteristics of love are evident in the poem above?

12. How do these characteristics compare with what Paul said about God's love?

BIBLE PASSAGE

"This is love: not that we loved God, but that he loved us and sent his Son as an atoning sacrifice for our sins. Dear friends, since God so loved us, we also ought to love one another. . . . And so we know and rely on the love God has for us.

"God is love. Whoever lives in love lives in God, and God in him. . . . We love because he first loved us. If anyone says, 'I love God,' yet hates his brother, he is a liar. For anyone who does not love his brother, whom he has seen, cannot love God, whom he has not seen" (1 John 4:10-11, 16, 19-20).

YOUR INSIGHTS

13. Why is it sometimes easier to say you love God than to actually show love to another human being?

14. How does God's coming to live on earth in the person of Jesus Christ set the example of true love?

15. If you agree with everything John says here, what relationships in your life will need some working on?

BIBLE PASSAGE

"It was just before the Passover Feast. Jesus knew that the time had come for him to leave this world and go to the Father. . . .[H]e poured water into a basin and began to wash his disciples' feet, drying them with the towel that was wrapped around him. . . . When he had finished washing their feet, he put on his clothes and returned to his place. 'Do you understand what I have done for you?' he asked them. 'You call me "Teacher" and "Lord," and rightly so, for that is what I am. Now that I, your Lord and Teacher, have washed your feet, you also should wash one another's feet' " (John 13:1, 5, 12-14).

YOUR INSIGHTS

16. What character qualities does Jesus demonstrate by washing His disciples' feet?

17. What are present-day equivalents to foot washing?

18. What people in your life need to see your love for them expressed in this way?

PRODIGALS AND THOSE WHO LOVE THEM

LOVE KNOWS WHAT TO DO

For my beloved I will not fear: Love knows what to do
For him, for her, from year to year, as hitherto;
Whom my heart cherishes are dear

To Thy heart too.

—Amy Carmichael in
Prodigals and Those Who Love Them

19. In your present situation, have you treated your prodigal as God has treated you?

20. In what concrete ways can you further show God's love to your prodigal?

SUMMARY

If we've experienced the unmerited favor of God's love, we need to attempt to show that same love to others, no matter what the cost.

LESSON FIVE

OBEDIENCE: OUR PRIVILEGE

AS A MOTHER, I MUST FAITHFULLY, PATIENTLY, LOVINGLY AND

HAPPILY DO MY PART—THEN QUIETLY WAIT FOR GOD TO DO HIS.

—RUTH BELL GRAHAM IN *PRODIGALS AND THOSE WHO LOVE THEM*

GOD COMMANDS NOTHING BUT WHAT IS BENEFICIAL.

"O ISRAEL, WHAT DOTH THE LORD REQUIRE OF THEE, BUT TO FEAR

THE LORD THY GOD. AND TO KEEP HIS STATUTES, WHICH I

COMMAND THEE THIS DAY, FOR THY GOOD?" TO OBEY GOD,

IS NOT SO MUCH OUR DUTY AS OUR PRIVILEGE.

—THOMAS WATSON, SIXTEENTH-CENTURY AUTHOR, IN *PRODIGALS AND THOSE WHO LOVE THEM*

SOMETIMES it's hard for us

to see obedience to God as important, especially when our minds are filled with worry for a prodigal. Yet, it is especially at those times that obedience to God can bear the most fruit. God expects obedience not only from those who have left or strayed from the path, but also from those who long and pray for the prodigal's return. Each of us can learn valuable lessons in the school of obedience.

Let God probe your own heart and situation as you consider the following passages.

BIBLE PASSAGES

"If anyone loves me, he will obey my teaching. My Father will love him, and we will come to him and make our home with him" (John 14: 23).

"If you obey my commands, you will remain in my love, just as I have obeyed my Father's commands and remain in his love" (John 15:10).

YOUR INSIGHTS

1. How is obedience to God an outgrowth of our love for Him?

2. Why is obedience necessary to the intimate relationship with God described in the above verses?

3. How can an intimate relationship with God help to restore broken family relationships?

BIBLE PASSAGE

"Therefore everyone who hears these words of mine and puts them into practice is like a wise man who built his house on the rock. The rain came down, the streams rose, and the wind blew and beat against that house; yet it did not fall, because it had its foundation on the rock. But everyone who hears these words of mine and does not put them into practice is like a foolish man who built his house on the sand. The rain came down, the streams rose, and the winds blew and beat against that house, and it fell with a great crash" (Matthew 7:24-27).

YOUR INSIGHTS

4. Who, according to the above passage, is the person who builds on sand?

5. How has your own life or family life at times been "built on sand"?

6. How can you begin to build on a solid rock?

7. Does the Bible offer any hope that a house built on sand can become a house built on rock? (See 2 Chronicles 7:14; Joel 2:25.)

8. How could obedience to each of the following biblical exhortations help you through your present family crisis?

"Pray continually" (1 Thessalonians 5:17).

"Give thanks in all circumstances" (1 Thessalonians 5:18).

"Love your enemies and pray for those who persecute you" (Matthew 5:44).

"Each of you should look not only to your own interests, but also to the interests of others" (Philippians 2:4).

"Therefore do not worry about tomorrow, for tomorrow will worry about itself. Each day has enough trouble of its own" (Matthew 6:34).

"Do not judge, or you too will be judged" (Matthew 7:1).

BIBLE PASSAGE

"Dear friends, if our hearts do not condemn us, we have confidence before God and receive from him anything we ask, because we obey his commands and do what pleases him. And this is his command: to believe in the name of his Son, Jesus Christ, and to love one another as he commanded us. Those who obey his commands live in him, and he in them" (1 John 3:21-24).

YOUR INSIGHTS

9. How can family problems cause our hearts to condemn us?

10. How does John say we can overcome this self-condemnation?

11. What two commands summarize God's desire for us?

12. What does God promise to those who live in obedience to Him?

13. How does this promise help us as we await the return of a prodigal?

14. How might obedience help us minister to a returned prodigal?

15. How can you love your prodigal more? How might you show the love you already have?

BIBLE PASSAGE

"By faith Noah, when warned about things not yet seen, in holy fear built an ark to save his family" (Hebrews 11:7; see also Genesis 6).

YOUR INSIGHTS

16. What is meant by the phrase "holy fear" in Hebrews 11:7? How did it lead Noah to a life of obedience to God?

17. Noah built the ark "to save his family." How can our obedience to God help "save" the prodigals in our lives? (See Deuteronomy 5:29.)

PRODIGALS AND THOSE WHO LOVE THEM

In "Settling Some Things With God" on page 21, Ruth Graham tells of the time she became aware that "it is unrealistic to ask the Lord to do in someone else's life that which we are unwilling for Him to do in ours."

18. What are the areas of your life that you need to work on with God? List them below. Put your worries about your prodigal "on hold," and start to settle these areas today. As Mrs. Graham found out, the load will be lifted, and peace will come.

Things I Need to Settle With God:

SUMMARY

The commands God has given us were provided for a purpose. Our own obedience to God's Word will not in and of itself solve all our problems, but God promised to be close to those who are obedient and to provide His peace.

LESSON SIX

GOD'S PRESENCE AND FAITHFULNESS

LORD, STILL

MY ANXIOUS HEART

TO CALM DELIGHT—

FOR THE GREAT SHEPHERD

WATCHES WITH ME

OVER MY FLOCK

BY NIGHT.

—FROM "WATCH O'ER MY FLOCK" BY RUTH BELL GRAHAM

IN *PRODIGALS AND THOSE WHO LOVE THEM*

G

OD wants to be with us, His people, during both our good times and bad. As Moses assured Israel, "The eternal God is your refuge, and underneath are the everlasting arms" (Deuteronomy 33:27). Let's discover how He is with us.

BIBLE PASSAGE

"Where can I go from your Spirit? Where can I flee from your presence? If I go up to the heavens, you are there; if I make my bed in the depths, you are there. If I rise on the wings of the dawn, if I settle on the far side of the sea, even there your hand will guide me, your right hand will hold me fast. If I say, 'Surely the darkness will hide me and the light become night around me,' even the darkness will not be dark to you; the night will shine like the day, for darkness is as light to you" (Psalm 139:7-12).

YOUR INSIGHTS

1. How does David express God's omnipresence in this psalm?

2. Does he really want to flee from God? How can you tell?

3. Recall a time you wanted to get away from God. What were the circumstances?

4. If you've never tried to run from God, why do you think others have? Does that give you a right to condemn them?

BIBLE PASSAGE

"God is our refuge and strength, an ever-present help in trouble. Therefore we will not fear, though the earth give way and the mountains fall into the heart of the sea, though its waters roar and foam and the mountains quake with their surging. . . . There is a river whose streams make glad the city of God, the holy place where the Most High dwells. God is within her, she will not fall; God will help her at break of day. Nations are in uproar, kingdoms fall; he lifts his voice, the earth melts. The LORD Almighty is with us; the God of Jacob is our fortress" (Psalm 46:1-7).

YOUR INSIGHTS

5. According to the above passage, what does God's presence mean to us during the storms of life?

6. One commentator suggests that the first part of the passage shows the turmoil of the world outside, while the second part shows the peace within the place where God dwells. Recall a time you experienced God's peace amid life's storms.

PRODIGALS AND THOSE WHO LOVE THEM

WATCH O'ER MY FLOCK

Like other shepherds
help me keep
watch o'er my flock by night;
mindful of each need,
each hurt, which might
lead one to stray—
each weakness
and each ill—
while others sleep
teach me to pray.
At night the wolves and leopards,
hungry and clever, prowl
in search of strays
and wounded; when they howl,
Lord, still
my anxious heart
to calm delight—
for the Great Shepherd
watches with me
over my flock
by night.

—Ruth Bell Graham

7. What does this poem suggest God has the knowledge and power to do? List at least three things.

8. In what ways is God's help meaningful to Mrs. Graham?

9. In your present crisis, how can God's help be meaningful to you?

BIBLE PASSAGE

"When you go to war against your enemies and see horses and chariots and an army greater than yours, do not be afraid of them, because the LORD your God, who brought you up out of Egypt, will be with you. When you are about to go into battle, the priest shall come forward and address the army. He shall say: 'Hear, O Israel, today you are going into battle against your enemies. Do not be fainthearted or afraid; do not be terrified or give way to panic before them. For the LORD your God is the one who goes with you to fight for you against your enemies to give you victory' " (Deuteronomy 20:1-4).

YOUR INSIGHTS

10. What words in this passage express God's presence with the Israelites in times of war?

11. What words describe how they are to respond to that presence?

12. How can this passage encourage you in the battles you face?

BIBLE PASSAGES

"Do not let your hearts be troubled. Trust in God; trust also in me. In my Father's house are many rooms; if it were not so, I would have told you. I am going there to prepare a place for you. And if I go and prepare a place for you, I will come back and take you to be with me that you also may be where I am. . . . And I will ask the Father, and he will give you another Counselor to be with you forever—the Spirit of truth. The world cannot accept him, because it neither sees him nor knows him. But you know him, for he lives with you and will be in you. . . . But the Counselor, the Holy Spirit, whom the Father will send in my name, will teach you all things and will remind you of everything I have said to you. Peace I leave with you;

my peace I give you. I do not give to you as the world gives. Do not let your hearts be troubled and do not be afraid" (John 14:1-3, 16-17, 26-27).

"Then Jesus came to them and said, 'All authority in heaven and on earth has been given to me. Therefore go and make disciples of all nations, baptizing them in the name of the Father and of the Son and of the Holy Spirit, and teaching them to obey everything I have commanded you. And surely I am with you always, to the very end of the age' " (Matthew 28:18-20).

YOUR INSIGHTS

13. In John 14, what did Jesus promise His disciples just before His crucifixion?

14. Why was He so concerned that they know He would someday return for them?

15. In Matthew 28, what did Jesus promise just before His ascension?

16. According to John 14, in what other way is God with us as we await Christ's return?

17. How close does John 14 say the Holy Spirit is to each of us? (See also Romans 8:9; 1 Corinthians 3:16.)

PRODIGALS AND THOSE WHO LOVE THEM

GREAT IS THY FAITHFULNESS

"Great is Thy faithfulness," O God my Father,
There is no shadow of turning with Thee;
Thou changest not, Thy compassions, they fail not:
As Thou hast been Thou forever wilt be.

Summer and winter, and springtime and harvest,
Sun, moon and stars in their courses above,
Join with all nature in manifold witness,
To Thy great faithfulness, mercy and love.

Pardon for sin and a peace that endureth,

Thy own dear presence to cheer and to guide;

Strength for today and bright hope for tomorrow,

Blessings all mine, with ten thousand beside!

"Great is Thy faithfulness!

Great is Thy faithfulness!"

Morning by morning new mercies I see;

All I have needed Thy hand hath provided—

"Great is Thy faithfulness," Lord, unto me!

—Thomas O. Chisholm

18. What new mercies of the Lord do you see today?

19. How can knowing of God's presence and faithfulness help you deal with your family crisis?

SUMMARY

Nothing is more comforting in times of crisis than to know that the very God who created and controls our universe desires close fellowship with us. His presence is a very real consolation.

CONQUERING ANXIETIES

HE DOES NOT GO ALONE

. . . . I SENSE HE IS ACCOMPANIED.

—FROM "HE DOES NOT GO ALONE" BY RUTH BELL GRAHAM

IN *PRODIGALS AND THOSE WHO LOVE THEM*

WHAT does it mean, on an everyday basis, for God to be present in the life of our prodigal? For Him to be present in our lives? What does it mean, as we face the challenges and trials of life, to know the Almighty is facing each of them with us? In this lesson are a few Scriptures that show what's in store when we're willing simply to abide in God's presence.

BIBLE PASSAGE

"I am the true vine, and my Father is the gardener. He cuts off every branch in me that bears no fruit, while every branch that does bear fruit he prunes so that it will be even more fruitful. . . . I am the vine; you are the branches. If a man remains in me and I in him, he will bear much fruit; apart from me you can do nothing" (John 15:1-2, 5).

YOUR INSIGHTS

1. How is our relationship with Christ similar to the relationship of the vine to the branches?

2. What does God promise to those who bear fruit?

3. If you are presently in a crisis situation, what kind of "fruit" do you need to see in your life?

4. What might God need to prune from your life for you to produce the fruit He wants?

5. What does the phrase "apart from Me you can do nothing" mean to you in your current situation?

BIBLE PASSAGE

"But the fruit of the Spirit is love, joy, peace, patience, kindness, goodness, faithfulness, gentleness and self-control. Against such things there is no law. Those who belong to Christ Jesus have crucified the sinful nature with its passions and desires. Since we live by the Spirit, let us keep in step with the Spirit" (Galatians 5:22-25).

YOUR INSIGHTS

6. In this passage, we have a specific list of fruit God wants to produce in our lives. Circle the character qualities that would be

especially helpful for you to have during your present family situation. Which of these were in your answer to question 3?

7. Why might these qualities be especially hard to cultivate during a time of stress? How can you overcome those difficulties?

8. Describe in your own words what it means to "keep in step with the Spirit."

PRODIGALS AND THOSE WHO LOVE THEM
FRETTING

How many mistakes I have made with the children because I was "fretting"—concerned to the point of worry. And invariably it prompted me to unwise action: sharpness, unfair punishment, unwise discipline . . . even my attitude and tone of voice.

But a mother who walks with God knows He only asks her to take care of the possible and to trust Him with the impossible; she does not need to fret.

—Ruth Bell Graham

9. In reviewing your actions with your prodigal, write down any unwise actions on your part you can recall.

10. What do you think it means to be "a mother who walks with God"?

11. How does fretting affect your relationship with the Lord?

BIBLE PASSAGES

"He who dwells in the shelter of the Most High will rest in the shadow of the Almighty. I will say of the LORD, 'He is my refuge and my fortress, my God, in whom I trust.' Surely he will save you from the fowler's snare and from the deadly pestilence. He will cover you with his feathers, and under his wings you will find refuge; his faithfulness will be your shield and rampart. You will not fear the terror of night, nor the arrow that flies by day" (Psalm 91:1-5).

"But now, this is what the LORD says—he who created you, O Jacob, he who formed you, O Israel: 'Fear not, for I have redeemed you; I have summoned you by name; you are mine. When you pass through the waters, I will be with you; and when you pass through the rivers, they will not sweep over you. When you walk through the fire, you will not be burned; the flames will not set you ablaze' " (Isaiah 43:1-2).

YOUR INSIGHTS

12. In what ways are the following descriptions of God's presence in Psalm 91 meaningful to you:

• **shelter of the Most High**

• **shadow of the Almighty**

• **my refuge**

• **my fortress**

• **cover you with his feathers**

13. In the passage from Isaiah, God promises to protect us during life's difficult times for a specific reason. What is it?

14. How can you correlate the dangers listed in Isaiah with the perils you are presently experiencing?

BIBLE PASSAGES

"I have set the LORD always before me. Because he is at my right hand, I will not be shaken. Therefore my heart is glad and my tongue rejoices; my body also will rest secure" (Psalm 16:8-9).

"The LORD is close to the brokenhearted and saves those who are crushed in spirit" (Psalm 34:18).

"Cast all your anxiety on him because he cares for you" (1 Peter 5:7).

YOUR INSIGHTS

15. What comfort does the psalmist offer in Psalm 16 to those who are "shaken"?

16. How can life crush our spirits (Psalm 34)? What does God promise in such times?

17. All three of these scriptures promise God is with us in our times of crisis. What do they say about our part in being aware of His presence?

18. Why is it so difficult to let go of depression, worry and anxiety?

PRODIGALS AND THOSE WHO LOVE THEM

HE DOES NOT GO ALONE

He does not go alone—
this gangling boy, all legs and arms;
awkward and gentle and so prone
to impulse judgment. What alarms
mothers at home, praying, sleepless, tense,
are all the "what-ifs" Satan sends
as though in glee. And still I sense
he is accompanied. One apprehends
Divine forethought, guidance and, when needed,
an Intervening Hand. So I would pray
in wondering gratitude, for having heeded
God's promise, I can praise today.

—Ruth Bell Graham

20. In what ways did Mrs. Graham feel God was accompanying her prodigal? What evidences of them might be seen in a prodigal's life?

21. How can you have the same assurance that God is protecting and watching over your prodigal?

SUMMARY

Assurance of God's presence can come if we commune with Him and place our trust in Him. Then we become aware of His feathers protecting us—and our beloved prodigals.

LISTEN, LORD: PRAYING FOR YOUR PRODIGAL

LISTEN, LORD,

A MOTHER'S PRAYING

LOW AND QUIET

—FROM "LISTEN, LORD" BY RUTH BELL GRAHAM

IN *PRODIGALS AND THOSE WHO LOVE THEM*

LISTEN, LORD

Listen, Lord,

a mother's praying

low and quiet:

listen, please.

Listen what her tears

are saying,

see her heart

upon its knees;

lift the load

from her bowed shoulders

till she sees

and understands,

You, Who hold

the worlds together,

hold her problems

in Your hands.

—Ruth Bell Graham from
Prodigals and Those Who Love Them

IN *Prodigals and Those Who Love Them*, Mrs. Graham talks much about prayer. Several of the poems, like the one above, are themselves prayers. Yet many of us struggle with prayer. If you are frustrated about a particular problem, however, prayer may be the most effective tool in finding a solution, or at least in easing your mind.

After reading the following passages and answering the questions, try to incorporate what you learn into your own prayers.

BIBLE PASSAGE

"Ask and it will be given to you; seek and you will find; knock and the door will be opened to you. For everyone who asks receives; he who seeks finds; and to him who knocks, the door will be opened.

"Which of you, if his son asks for bread, will give him a stone? Or if he asks for a fish, will give him a snake? If you, then, though you are evil, know how to give good gifts to your children, how much more will your Father in heaven give good gifts to those who ask him!" (Matthew 7:7-11).

YOUR INSIGHTS

1. How can the above passage give you the confidence to pray for the things you need?

2. What is God's part in prayer, and what is ours?

3. How does our generosity compare to God's in answering our prayers?

4. Which best describes what God will give us in answer to our prayers:

___Less than we request

___Exactly what we request

___More than we request

PRODIGALS AND THOSE WHO LOVE THEM

It is often hard to understand how God answers prayer. Sometimes He doesn't give us what we ask for. Read the chapter on Augustine in *Prodigals and Those Who Love Them,* and answer the following questions:

5. What did Monica (Augustine's mother) ask God for in her prayers? (See page 8.)

6. How was Monica's prayer answered even though Augustine sailed to Rome?

7. What does Augustine mean when he says, "In the depth of Your counsels and hearing the main point of her desire, [You regarded] not what she then asked, that You [might] make me what she ever asked"?

Read "Persistence and Patience" on page 16, as well as "Had I Been Joseph's Mother" on page 69.

8. Recall one instance from your past in which you prayed for a specific event to happen and God chose to do something different. How did you feel about it at the time? How do you feel about it now? Why?

9. Think of a request you have been making to God that He has not yet answered. Ask Him for the faith to believe He will do something better than you can imagine.

10. How can you give God room in your prayers to "regard not what you now ask" but "what you ever ask"?

BIBLE PASSAGE

"In the same way, the Spirit helps us in our weakness. We do not know what we ought to pray for, but the Spirit himself intercedes for us with groans that words cannot express" (Romans 8:26).

YOUR INSIGHTS

11. What does Paul advise we do when we don't know what to ask for?

12. According to this verse, what is our condition that causes us to require the Spirit's help?

13. What sort of circumstances leave you not knowing how to pray? Why are these the most important petitions to bring to God?

BIBLE PASSAGE

"I will ask the Father, and he will give you another Counselor to be with you forever—the Spirit of truth. The world cannot accept him, because it neither sees him nor knows him. But you know him, for he lives with you and will be in you. . . . But the Counselor, the Holy Spirit, whom the Father will send in my name, will teach you all things and will remind you of everything I have said to you. Peace I leave with you; my peace I give you. I do not give to you as the world gives. Do not let your hearts be troubled and do not be afraid" (John 14:16-17, 26-27).

YOUR INSIGHTS

14. According to the above verses, how does the Holy Spirit intercede for us when we pray?

15. What does He accomplish in our lives as we pray?

PRODIGALS AND THOSE WHO LOVE THEM

SUNK IN THIS GRAY DEPRESSION

Sunk in this gray
depression
I cannot pray.
How can I give
expression
when there're no words
to say?
This mass of vague
foreboding
of aching care,
love with its
overloading
short-circuits prayer.
Then through this fog
of tiredness,
this nothingness, I find
only a quiet knowing
that He is kind.

—Ruth Bell Graham from
Prodigals and Those Who Love Them

16. Underline the emotions you relate to in Mrs. Graham's poem. List any other emotions you feel right now.

17. Ask God to help you know that He is kind to you, even when you're hurting.

BIBLE PASSAGE—YOUR INSIGHTS

18. Describe in one or two words the attitudes exemplified by each prayer below. Underline the attitudes that need to be more a part of your prayer life.

• "Far be it from me that I should sin against the Lord by failing to pray for you" (1 Samuel 12:23a).

• "Hear my cry for mercy as I call to you for help, as I lift up my hands toward your Most Holy Place" (Psalm 28:2).

• "Praise be to the Lord, for he has heard my cry for mercy" (Psalm 28:6).

• "Because he turned his ear to me, I will call on him as long as I live" (Psalm 116:2).

•"Out of the depths I cry to you, O Lord" (Psalm 130:1).

• "O Lord, listen! O Lord, forgive! O Lord, hear and act!" (Daniel 9:19a).

• "Yet not my will, but yours be done" (Luke 22:42b).

19. **The Bible contains many promises for those who take the time to pray. What do each of the following verses promise? Put a star by those you need to depend on for your present situation.**

• "For he will deliver the needy who cry out, the afflicted who have no one to help" (Psalm 72:12).

• "He will call upon me, and I will answer him; I will be with him in trouble, I will deliver him and honor him" (Psalm 91:15).

• "Before they call I will answer; while they are still speaking I will hear" (Isaiah 65:24).

• "You will seek me and find me when you seek me with all your heart" (Jeremiah 29:13).

• "If any of you lacks wisdom, he should ask God, who gives generously to all without finding fault, and it will be given to him" (James 1:5).

BIBLE PASSAGE

"Do not be anxious about anything, but in everything, by prayer and petition, with thanksgiving, present your requests to God. And the peace of God, which transcends all understanding, will guard your hearts and your minds in Christ Jesus" (Philippians 4:6-7).

YOUR INSIGHTS

20. In what way is prayer the answer to anxiety?

21. Why is thanksgiving an important part of prayer?

22. How can giving thanks help us see beyond any problems that are weighing us down?

23. What does God promise to those who pray with thanksgiving?

PRODIGALS AND THOSE WHO LOVE THEM

After reading Philippians 4:6-7, Mrs. Graham "suddenly. . .realized the missing ingredient in my prayers had been 'with thanksgiving.' So I put down my Bible and spent time worshiping Him for who He and what He is. This covers more territory than any mortal can comprehend. Even contemplating what little we do know dissolves doubts, reinforces faith and restores joy.

"I began to thank God for giving me this one I loved so dearly in the first place. I even thanked Him for the difficult spots which taught me so much.

"And you know what happened? It was as if someone turned on the lights in my mind and heart, and the little fears and worries that had been nibbling away in the darkness like mice and cockroaches hurriedly scuttled for cover."

Read the entire article "Worship and Worry" on page 39 in *Prodigals and Those Who Love Them.*

24. In your present situation, list the things for which you can give thanks.

25. Write down which of God's attributes you've seen Him express at various times in your life.

SUMMARY

"Stonewall Jackson," says E. M. Bounds in *Purpose in Prayer,* "was a man of prayer. Said he, 'I have so fixed the habit of prayer in my mind that I never raise a glass of water to my lips without asking God's blessing, never seal a letter without putting a word of prayer under the seal, and never change my classes in the lecture-room without a minute's petition for the cadets who go out and for those who come in.' "

His life is a good example of what Paul meant by "pray continually" (1 Thessalonians 5:17), a habit from which all of us would benefit.

OUR BOUNDLESS GOD: UNDERSTANDING HIS POWER

POOR PRODIGAL! SEEKING A "WHERE" FROM "WHENCE,"

HOW DOES ONE ESCAPE OMNIPOTENCE?

—FROM "FLEEING FROM YOU" BY RUTH BELL GRAHAM

IN *PRODIGALS AND THOSE WHO LOVE THEM*

THE power of God to work in any situation is a theme woven throughout *Prodigals and Those Who Love Them.* Mrs. Graham quotes Mrs. Charles Cowman as saying, "Our vital need is for a vital faith in God—in the omnipotent God. When oppressed with staggering problems, do not consider their boundaries but rediscover the boundlessness of God."

Perhaps our greatest comfort in a time of crisis is simply knowing that God is in control. This is commonly referred to as the sovereignty of God, and it is a dominant theme throughout God's Book. Remember, the God we're reading about in the following passages is the same God who watches over you and your prodigal.

BIBLE PASSAGE

"Moses said to God, 'Suppose I go to the Israelites and say to them, "The God of your fathers has sent me to you," and they ask me, "What is his name?" Then what shall I tell them?'

"God said to Moses, 'I AM WHO I AM. This is what you are to say to the Israelites: "I AM has sent me to you" ' " (Exodus 3:13-14).

YOUR INSIGHTS

1. What does the name I AM tell us about God? How does it express His sovereignty?

2. Read John 8:58, where Jesus gives Himself the same name. What does that tell us about Jesus?

3. What implications does that name have in God's relationship with you?

BIBLE PASSAGE

" 'This is what is decreed for you, King Nebuchadnezzar: Your royal authority has been taken from you. You will be driven away from people and will live with the wild animals; you will eat grass like cattle. Seven times will pass by for you until you acknowledge that the Most High is sovereign over the kingdoms of men and gives them to anyone he wishes.'

"Immediately what had been said about Nebuchadnezzar was fulfilled. He was driven away from people and ate grass like cattle. His body was drenched with the dew of heaven until his hair grew like the feathers of an eagle and his nails like the claws of a bird.

"At the end of that time, I, Nebuchadnezzar, raised my eyes toward heaven, and my sanity was restored. Then I praised the Most High; I honored and glorified him who lives forever.

"His dominion is an eternal dominion; his kingdom endures from generation to generation. All the peoples of the earth are regarded as nothing. He does as he pleases with the powers of heaven and the peoples of the earth. No one can hold back his hand or say to him: 'What have you done?' " (Daniel 4:31b-35).

YOUR INSIGHTS

4. Skim Daniel 1-4 to learn the full story of God's dealings with King Nebuchadnezzar. What was his attitude toward God after his ordeal?

5. What main truth did he learn about God?

6. Daniel 4:36 says Nebuchadnezzar's "sanity was restored" after this ordeal. How can acknowledgment of God's sovereignty give us mental stability amid perplexing situations?

7. What important truths have you learned about God through crises?

BIBLE PASSAGES

"The LORD does whatever pleases him, in the heavens and on the earth, in the seas and all their depths" (Psalm 135:6).

"The LORD is righteous in all his ways and loving toward all he has made" (Psalm 145:17).

YOUR INSIGHTS

8. What phrase in Psalm 135:6 echoes what Nebuchadnezzar said about God?

9. What does Psalm 145 tell us our sovereign God "pleases" to do?

10. If you could provide an answer to your present crisis, what would it be?

11. Write a prayer in which you let God know you ultimately want His wisdom to prevail.

PRODIGALS AND THOSE WHO LOVE THEM

HAD I BEEN JOSEPH'S MOTHER

Had I been Joseph's mother
I'd have prayed
protection from his brothers
"God, keep him safe.
He is so young,
so different from
the others."
Mercifully,
she never knew
there would be slavery
and prison, too.

Had I been Moses' mother
I'd have wept
to keep my little son:
praying she might forget
the babe drawn from the water
of the Nile.
Had I not kept
him for her
nursing him the while,
was he not mine?
—and she
but Pharaoh's daughter?

Had I been Daniel's mother
I should have pled
"Give victory!
—this Babylonian horde
godless and cruel—
Don't let him be a captive
—better dead,
Almighty Lord!"

Had I been Mary,
Oh, had I been she,
I would have cried
as never mother cried,
"Anything, O God,
Anything . . .
—but
crucified."

With such prayers importunate
my finite wisdom would assail
Infinite Wisdom.
God, how fortunate
Infinite Wisdom
should prevail.

—Ruth Bell Graham in
Prodigals and Those Who Love Them

89

BIBLE PASSAGE

"The LORD Almighty has sworn, 'Surely, as I have planned, so it will be, and as I have purposed, so it will stand. I will crush the Assyrian in my land; on my mountains I will trample him down. His yoke will be taken from my people, and his burden removed from their shoulders.'

"This is the plan determined for the whole world; this is the hand stretched out over all nations. For the LORD Almighty has purposed, and who can thwart him? His hand is stretched out, and who can turn it back?" (Isaiah 14:24-27).

YOUR INSIGHTS

12. What does this passage teach about God's control over the events of history?

13. How does this truth relate to the everyday events of your own life?

BIBLE PASSAGE

"But Joseph said to them, 'Don't be afraid. Am I in the place of God? You intended to harm me, but God intended it for good to accomplish what is now being done, the saving of many lives' " (Genesis 50:19-20).

YOUR INSIGHTS

14. How does Mrs. Graham see her wisdom compared to God's wisdom in "Had I Been Joseph's Mother"?

15. Genesis 37-50 tells the amazing story of Joseph. From what you know of his story, how does his statement that "God meant it for good" summarize God's oversight of human events?

16. Joseph admits his brothers meant to harm him. Describe a time when you saw God's care for you, even though the people around you didn't have your best interests in mind?

17. How did Joseph develop his trust in God's sovereignty?

PRODIGALS AND THOSE WHO LOVE THEM
SOVEREIGN OR NOT?

"The fool hath said in his heart, There is no God."

—Psalm 14:1

This goes also for those who doubt His sovereignty. Either He is sovereign or He is not. If He is not sovereign, He is not God. Therefore, when we become so preoccupied with and dismayed by circumstances and certain people that we doubt God's ability to handle things His own way in His own time, then we, too, are fools.

—Ruth Bell Graham note on Psalm 14:1, July 1, 1965

18. In what ways have you doubted God's sovereignty in your present situation?

19. How can you regain a sense of His power?

SUMMARY

Just as a king is sovereign in his kingdom, so God is ultimately in control of everything that happens in His creation. If we keep in mind that God can do anything, we can have hope no matter how troubled the situation.

LESSON TEN

ENTRUSTING OUR LOVED ONES TO GOD

THE LORD WHO HAS BEEN KIND TO ME

WILL NOT BE LESS SO TO THEM.

—FROM ISOBEL KUHN IN *PRODIGALS AND THOSE WHO LOVE THEM*

DYING of cancer, Isobel Kuhn wrote in *In the Arena,* "The future of my loved ones after I leave them? The Lord who has been kind to me will not be less so to them."

When we face crisis situations, we can turn to any number of places for help. We can seek the advice of competent professionals; we can rely on the support and wisdom of trusted friends or family members; we can even fall back on our own wisdom and common sense. But we must at all times remember to trust God.

BIBLE PASSAGE

"And we know that in all things God works for the good of those who love him, who have been called according to his purpose. For those God foreknew he also predestined to be conformed to the likeness of his Son, that he might be the firstborn among many brothers. And those he predestined, he also called; those he called, he also justified; those he justified, he also glorified" (Romans 8:28-30).

YOUR INSIGHTS

1. How does the opening promise of this passage depend on God's sovereign control of the universe?

2. According to that promise, what two things have to be true of us if we're to see God working for our good in all things?

3. How should the rest of the passage affect our sense of security as God's children?

4. What do these verses say about God's concern for the details of our lives?

BIBLE PASSAGE

"Perhaps the reason he was separated from you for a little while was that you might have him back for good—no longer as a slave, but better than a slave, as a dear brother" (Philemon 15-16a).

YOUR INSIGHTS

5. When Philemon's slave Onesimus ran away, he met Paul, who led him to faith in Christ. How does Paul see this as an example of God's sovereignty? (Read the whole book—it's only twenty-five verses long!)

6. List prodigals you know who turned into disciples. If you can't think of any you know personally, ask your friends. This list can be a source of encouragement to you.

7. What does Paul's counsel in the book of Philemon suggest about how you should relate to your prodigal?

PRODIGALS AND THOSE WHO LOVE THEM

As for Monica, her work on earth was done. One day shortly after Augustine's conversion, she announced to him that she had nothing left to live for, now that she had achieved her lifelong quest of seeing him come to faith in Christ. Just nine days later, she died.

—From "Aurelius Augustine"

Read the story of Augustine from *Prodigals and Those Who Love Them.*

PERSISTENCE AND PATIENCE

How often has God said no to my earnest prayers that He might answer my deepest longings, give me something more, something better?

One's heart goes out to Monica, praying so desperately, so persistently for her brilliant, wayward son. It was over thirty years before God answered.

This is one more illustration that when I am dealing with an all-powerful, all-knowing God, I, as a mere mortal, must offer my petitions not only with persistence but also with patience. Someday I'll know why.

—Ruth Bell Graham

8. In what ways was Monica comforted during the years of praying for her son?

9. When Monica approached her church leaders about the problem, what was their response?

10. What would help you to show the same persistence and patience?

BIBLE PASSAGES

"I am still confident of this: I will see the goodness of the LORD in the land of the living. Wait for the LORD; be strong and take heart and wait for the LORD" (Psalm 27:13-14).

"Even youths grow tired and weary, and young men stumble and fall; but those who hope in the LORD will renew their strength. They will soar on wings like eagles; they will run and not grow weary, they will walk and not be faint" (Isaiah 40:30-31).

YOUR INSIGHTS

12. According to these two scriptures, how we can demonstrate that we trust in God's sovereignty?

13. The psalmist said he was confident he would see the "goodness of the Lord." Briefly look over the rest of this psalm; what do you think his life was like when he wrote these words?

14. What happens to the person who is confident in God's goodness?

15. How can the promises of the Isaiah passage help when you feel weighed down by life's problems?

BIBLE PASSAGE

"And let us not be weary in well doing; for in due season we shall reap, if we faint not" (Galatians 6:9, KJV).

YOUR INSIGHTS

16. How is our ability to persevere affected by our level of trust in God's sovereignty?

17. What kinds of "well-doing" can you be involved in as you wait to reap God's promises?

PRODIGALS AND THOSE WHO LOVE THEM

A turn of the path brought her within sight of the cottage, and her heart came into her mouth, for the kitchen window was ablaze with light. One moment she feared Lachlan might be ill, but in the next she understood, and in the greatness of her joy, she ran the rest of the way.

—From "Flora Campbell"

PRODIGALS AND THOSE WHO LOVE THEM

Read the story of Flora Campbell. Then read John 16:8 and "The Possible and the Impossible."

THE POSSIBLE AND THE IMPOSSIBLE

We mothers must take care of the possible and trust God for the impossible. We are to love, affirm, encourage, teach, listen and care for the physical needs of the family.

We cannot convict of sin, create hunger and thirst after God, or convert. These are miracles, and miracles are not in our department.

My Part (the possible):	**God's Part** (the impossible):
love—love expressed	conviction of sin
to pray intelligently	creating a hunger
logically	and thirst for
urgently	righteousness
without ceasing	conversion
in faith	bringing to the place
enjoy being a mother	of total commitment
provide a warm, happy home	showing us ourselves
minister to their physical	as we really are
and emotional needs	(without ever
as I am able	discouraging us!)
	continually filling us with
	His Holy Spirit for
	our sanctification
	and His service

18. List the things you can do in your present situation. Then, beside them, list the things you must let God do.

My Part   God's Part

SUMMARY

Whatever human means of emotional support we seek, we should not forget the wisdom, strength and security that are ours as beloved children of a sovereign God. In the final analysis, we must trust Him.

HIS WAYS ARE NOT OUR WAYS

HOW FORTUNATE INFINITE WISDOM SHOULD PREVAIL.

—FROM "HAD I BEEN JOSEPH'S MOTHER" BY RUTH BELL GRAHAM

IN *PRODIGALS AND THOSE WHO LOVE THEM*

THE more we become aware of God's sovereignty over all aspects of His creation and over us as His creatures, the more we realize that His ways are not our ways and "Father knows best."

BIBLE PASSAGE

"Then the LORD sent a great wind on the sea, and such a violent storm arose that the ship threatened to break up. All the sailors were afraid and each cried out to his own god. And they threw the cargo into the sea to lighten the ship.

"But Jonah had gone below deck, where he lay down and fell into a deep sleep. The captain went to him and said, 'How can you sleep? Get up and call on your god! Maybe he will take notice of us, and we will not perish.'

"Then the sailors said to each other, 'Come, let us cast lots to find out who is responsible for this calamity.' They cast lots and the lot fell on Jonah.

"So they asked him, 'Tell us, who is responsible for making all this trouble for us? What do you do? Where do you come from? What is your country? From what people are you?'

"He answered, 'I am a Hebrew and I worship the LORD, the God of heaven, who made the sea and the land.'

"This terrified them and they asked, 'What have you done?' (They knew he was running away from the LORD, because he had already told them so.)

"The sea was getting rougher and rougher. So they asked him, 'What should we do to you to make the sea calm down for us?'

" 'Pick me up and throw me into the sea,' he replied, 'and it will become calm. I know that it is my fault that this great storm has come upon you.'

"Instead, the men did their best to row back to land. But they could not, for the sea grew even wilder than before. Then they cried to the LORD, 'O LORD, please do not let us die for taking this man's life. Do not hold us accountable for killing an innocent man, for you, O LORD, have done as you pleased.' Then they took Jonah and threw him overboard, and the raging sea grew calm. At this the men greatly feared the LORD, and they offered a sacrifice to the LORD and made vows to him.

"But the LORD provided a great fish to swallow Jonah, and Jonah was inside the fish three days and three nights" (Jonah 1:4-17, see also the remainder of the book).

YOUR INSIGHTS

1. When Jonah was thrown overboard, what did the sailors think would become of him?

2. What were Jonah's thoughts as he fell deeper in the water (Jonah 2:2-7)?

3. Do you agree that God had to take drastic measures to bring Jonah to his senses? Why or why not? What does this tell you about how God sometimes works in people's lives?

4. How did God continue to have trouble with Jonah even after Jonah quit running away (Jonah 4)? What does this tell you about a returned prodigal?

5. Based on Jonah's story, when do you think a prodigal is too far gone?

PRODIGALS AND THOSE WHO LOVE THEM

MOSES' WANDERINGS WEREN'T ALL FOR NAUGHT

Moses' wanderings weren't
all for naught:

Wandering, he learned the
wilderness first hand;
And later through this
Devastation brought

His brethren from bondage to
the Promised Land.

—Ruth Bell Graham

6. What wandering of Moses' does this poem refer to? (See Exodus 2:11-3:17.)

7. What was Moses' sin?

8. Did his sin or his running away ruin his life? Why or why not?

BIBLE PASSAGE

"I cried out to God for help; I cried out to God to hear me. When I was in distress, I sought the LORD; at night I stretched out untiring hands and my soul refused to be comforted. I remembered you, O God, and I groaned; I mused, and my spirit grew faint.

"You kept my eyes from closing; I was too troubled to speak. I thought about the former days, the years of long ago; I remembered my songs in the night. My heart mused and my spirit inquired: 'Will the LORD reject forever? Will he never show his favor again? Has his unfailing love vanished forever? Has his promise failed for all time? Has God forgotten to be merciful? Has he in anger withheld his compassion?'

"Then I thought, 'To this I will appeal: the years of the right hand of the Most High.' I will remember the deeds of the LORD; yes, I will remember your miracles of long ago. I will meditate on all your works and consider all your mighty deeds.

"Your ways, O God, are holy. What god is so great as our God? You are the God who performs miracles; you display your power among the peoples. With your mighty arm you redeemed your people, the descendants of Jacob and Joseph" (Psalm 77:1-15).

YOUR INSIGHTS

9. State the theme of this psalm in your own words. How does this passage relate to the other passages reviewed in this lesson?

10. When the psalmist began to write this psalm, he seemed anxious and depressed. What thoughts changed his attitude as he continued to write?

11. Why is it sometimes hard for you to believe that, in your situation, God can still perform miracles?

PRODIGALS AND THOSE WHO LOVE THEM
Read John Newton's story in *Prodigals and Those Who Love Them.*

12. How was Newton's sinful past used for God's greater glory in later years?

13. How do you feel about William Jay's statement, "If he be [a penitent], I shall never despair of the conversion of anyone again"?

BIBLE PASSAGE

"Oh, the depth of the riches of the wisdom and knowledge of God! How unsearchable his judgments, and his paths beyond tracing out! 'Who has known the mind of the Lord? Or who has been his counselor?' 'Who has ever given to God, that God should repay him?' For from him and through him and to him are all things. To him be the glory forever! Amen" (Romans 11:33-36).

YOUR INSIGHTS

14. Paul penned these words after writing nine chapters of the deepest theological insights to be found anywhere in the Bible. In light of this, why are Paul's words so remarkable?

15. How would you describe Paul's attitude toward God?

16. Write a paragraph about your own view of God. Offer it to Him as a praise and a prayer.

Summary

Never give up hope! Throughout the Bible, God turned lives around and brought forth great good from what appeared to be hopeless cases. He can do that today as well.

PROCLAIMING HIS GRACE: REACHING OUT TO OTHERS

BUT IN HIS DUTY, PROMPT AT EVERY CALL, HE WATCHED

AND WEPT, HE PRAYED AND FELT FOR ALL.

—ABOUT JOHN NEWTON FROM *PRODIGALS AND THOSE WHO LOVE THEM*

YEARS ago, a missionary doctor to China cured a man of cataracts. A few weeks later, forty-eight blind men came to the doctor. They were all holding on to a rope, guided by the man who had been cured. He had led them, walking in a chain, for more than 250 miles.

Because we have received God's saving grace, we should be motivated, like the man who received his sight, to share the good news of His grace with the people He brings into our lives. Sometimes this means telling a person who has never heard the claims of Christ; in other cases it means reminding forgetful or unfaithful believers of truths they already know. It may even mean going out to find particular lost souls.

BIBLE PASSAGE

"God was reconciling the world to himself in Christ, not counting men's sins against them. And he has committed to us the message of reconciliation. We are therefore Christ's ambassadors, as though God were making his appeal through us. We implore you on Christ's behalf: Be reconciled to God" (2 Corinthians 5:19-20).

YOUR INSIGHTS

1. Why do we have a responsibility to proclaim the gospel?

2. What does it mean to you to be an ambassador of Christ?

3. What is involved in our being reconciled to God? How can we help other people experience such reconciliation?

4. How can peace with God lead to the healing of human relationships?

BIBLE PASSAGE

"If a man owns a hundred sheep, and one of them wanders away, will he not leave the ninety-nine on the hills and go to look for the one that wandered off? And if he finds it, I tell you the truth, he is happier about that one sheep than about the ninety-nine that did not wander off. In the same way your Father in heaven is not willing that any of these little ones should be lost" (Matthew 18:12-14).

YOUR INSIGHTS

5. What does this story teach us about God's concern for those who have never responded to His offer of eternal life, or who have wandered away from Him?

6. What does the last sentence of this passage mean to you as you think of your own prodigal?

7. Besides your prodigal, who are the lost sheep in your own life whom you can pursue?

8. How do you balance your efforts on behalf of the lost sheep with the ongoing needs of those who have not wandered?

BIBLE PASSAGES

"Let your light shine before men, that they may see your good deeds and praise your Father in heaven" (Matthew 5:16).

"In the same way, you wives, be submissive to your own husbands so that even if any of them are disobedient to the word they may be won without a word by the behavior of their wives, as they observe your chaste and respectful behavior" (1 Peter 3:1-2, NASB).

YOUR INSIGHTS

9. How can we "let our light shine" without verbally declaring our faith?

10. When has such a "silent witness" been necessary in your own life? Whom have you seen come to faith in Christ as a result?

11. How can you know when it is time to break the silence in such a relationship?

12. Why is it often best to witness without a word in the case of a prodigal husband or wife?

PRODIGALS AND THOSE WHO LOVE THEM
"What do you do this for?". . . "To find you."

—From "The Lost Doctor"

Read the story of the lost doctor in *Prodigals and Those Who Love Them.*

13. Among those you are praying for, who could benefit from your talking to them directly?

14. Whom can you minister to in other ways?

15. Instead of being discouraged by the many lost souls in London who did not come to the church for answers, George Dempster

decided to go out to find them. How can you help others who have prodigals or who are on the run from either God or their families?

BIBLE PASSAGE

"My brothers, if one of you should wander from the truth and someone should bring him back, remember this: Whoever turns a sinner from the error of his way will save him from death and cover over a multitude of sins" (James 5:19-20).

YOUR INSIGHTS

16. Does this passage imply we should always go after the one who wanders? Why or why not?

17. What examples in Scripture can you think of in which the wanderer was not aggressively pursued? What was the ultimate outcome?

BIBLE PASSAGE

"So I will always remind you of these things, even though you know them and are firmly established in the truth you now have. I think it is right to refresh your memory as long as I live in the tent of this body" (2 Peter 1:12-13).

YOUR INSIGHTS

18. As Peter states, he has just preached the gospel to some people who already know it well (see verses 1-11). Why is it important to continually remind each other of what God has done for us in Christ?

PRODIGALS AND THOSE WHO LOVE THEM

Read the story of Flora Campbell, if you have not already done so.

19. Who reached out to minister to Flora? Who else played a part in helping Flora find her way home?

20. What was the tone of the letter to Flora?

21. What can you learn from the action of Marget Howe in dealing with your own prodigal?

SUMMARY

Many of God's children who are lost are scattered throughout the world—and many more are on the lookout for the lost. Throughout *Prodigals and Those Who Love Them,* these folk have appeared in all the main stories—sometimes as major characters like George Dempster, who went in search of prodigals; sometimes as brief, one-time contacts like the two women who slipped Dostoyevski a New Testament.

Their examples should encourage you to pray that God will use someone to reach out to your prodigal. At the same time, why not reach out yourself to those nearby who are hurting and may also be prodigals?

TEACHER'S NOTES

The number of lessons in this book is designed so that it can be used in a regular Sunday school quarter. The thirteenth lesson can be either a review or a continuation of any one particular lesson. This material could also benefit two people going over it together or an individual working through it alone.

But studying these lessons with a group can help accomplish several things: 1) A group may help some people realize that others are suffering in the same way they are. 2) Group members encourage one another. 3) Groups can also help to keep us from misinterpretation.

When leading a group, always start on time and begin with prayer. The Holy Spirit gives us understanding, so ask Him for that at the outset. Ask the others to bring their Bibles, pen and paper. Writing things down is not only therapeutic, but it also helps memory retention.

Try to involve everyone. Those who are hurting may find it difficult to interact on this topic. Be sensitive, and pray for discernment. Your ability to draw people into the discussion may be the most important thing you can accomplish.

Keep the conversation relaxed. Emphasize that no question is bad or not worth asking. Listen carefully, be affirming, and take every question seriously.

If you don't know an answer, admit it. Encourage the group to consider, pray about and study the question during the next week.

Above all, attempt to be a source of encouragement to one another.